Amir's
BIG CATCH

by Sheila Jones & Charis Haines
illustrated by Kevin Cannon

Edited by Lily Coyle
Illustrated by Kevin Cannon

Special thanks to Anielle D. for your time and creative input at the start of Amir's story

ISBN 13: 978-1-59298-637-8
Library of Congress Catalog Number: 2016912189
Printed in the United States of America
First Printing: 2017
21 20 19 18 17   5 4 3 2 1

Cover and interior design by Kevin Cannon

Beaver's Pond Press, Inc.
7108 Ohms Lane
Edina, MN 55439–2129
(952) 829-8818
www.BeaversPondPress.com

To order, visit www.ItascaBooks.com
or call (800) 901-3480. Reseller discounts available.

www.AmirsBigCatch.com

This book belongs to _____

My first fish was caught on _____

Type of fish _____

I went fishing with _____

Amir lived by a lake.

Every day he tried to catch a fish with his hands, but they just swam away.

Felix was flexy and Lani was lengthy.

Felix was flexy,
Lani was lengthy,
Wes was wiggly,
Ted was tricky,
and Hattie was handy—
but Sage was sturdy and
Bella was bouncy.

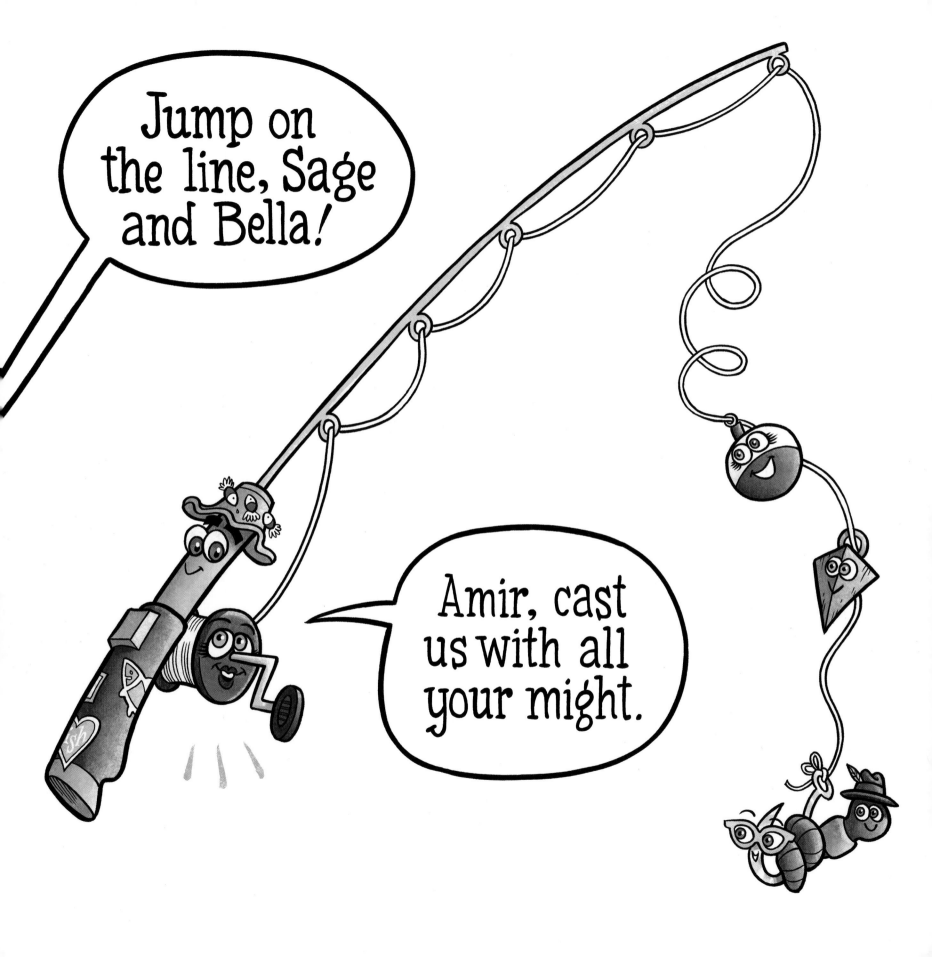

Felix was flexy, Lani was lengthy, Wes was wiggly, Ted was tricky, Hattie was handy, Sage was sturdy, Bella was bouncy—and Amir was friendly.